# FENCING THROUGH THE AGES

# FENCING THROUGH THE AGES

# *L'ESCRIME À TRAVERS LES ÂGES*

ADOLPHE CORTHEY

translated Chris Slee

Fencing through the Ages

Copyright © 2015 Chris Slee (translator)

ISBN: 978-0-9943590-1-8 (eBook)

ISBN: 978-0-9943590-0-1 (Print)

All Rights Reserved.  No part of this publication may be reproduced, stored in a retrieval system, or transmitted, in any form or in any means – by electronic, mechanical, photocopying, recording or otherwise – without prior written permission from the copyright owner(s).

*L'Escrime à travers les Âges*, Adolphe Corthey. Original text is based on the 1898 edition. It is asserted this book is in the public domain.

*Rapport du Comité de la Société d'Encouragement de l'Escrime au Sujet de la Transformation de l'Épée de Combat*, Adolphe Corthey. Original text is based on the 1894 edition. It is asserted this book is in the public domain.

It is asserted that the individual articles and extracts from *Le Sport en France et à l'Etranger, La Presse, Le Figaro, Gil Blas, Le Monde Illustre, Revue Illustrée* are in the public domain.

Cover illustration from an advertising flyer for "*Séance d'Escrime Offerte au Profit des Pauvres*" (1895)

Created at PressBooks.com for LongEdge Press, First edition

*To Kathi and Henry,
Charlotte and Marianne*

# Contents

Introduction ..... 1

## Adolphe Corthey
Ad. Corthey - Silhouette Sportif ..... 9

## Fencing through the Ages
Preface ..... 15
I ..... 19
II ..... 21
III ..... 27
IV ..... 31
V ..... 37
VI ..... 43

## Press Reports
At the Circus Molier ..... 51
A Clown's Report from the Circus Molier ..... 53
The Society for the Advancement of Fencing ..... 57
Letter from Belgium ..... 61

## On the Subject of the Transformation of the Combat Sword
Report of the Committee ..... 65

# Introduction

This book started as a simple translation of Corthey's <u>Fencing through the Ages</u> and grew into something approaching a study of the man through his works. Corthey is one of the great men of nineteenth century fencing and of what has been termed the first HEMA revival who has gone largely unnoticed by the English-speaking and unfortunately by French-speaking HEMA communities.

The silhouette of Adolphe Corthey given in *Le Sport en France et à l'Étranger* was published in the year before his death and shows a keen sportsman skilled in shooting, archery and fencing, active until his final days. By trade, he started in the law and at some point gave that away to write for the Parisian stage where he achieved a degree of fame for his satires and comedies. His sporting career started early with gymnastics and, until he relocated from Switzerland to France, canoeing. He was well known as a writer on military topics and proposed several improvements on then current weapons for the military and in more sporting contexts, including a complete redesign of the then standard-issue bayonet and a proposal for bringing duelling closer to sport fencing by altering the weapon. Corthey was a skilled fencer and is in every way the French-speaking world's equivalent to Alfred Hutton or Egerton Castle. His obituaries, some of which are included in this volume, show a man well loved and respected within all the circles, professional and amateur, in which he moved. He seems to have been genuinely liked and appreciated by all who had dealings with him.

Corthey was for at least one term secretary of the Society for the Advancement of Fencing[1] and it is for this body that both works included here were written. The Society was founded in 1882 by H. Hébrard de Villeneuve, a veteran of the War of 1870 and himself a fencer of some repute. Villeneuve organised the international fencing competitions of 1896-7 and the fencing exhibitions of the Great Exposition of 1900 and was a member of the International Olympic Committee for over a decade. The Society joined with the National Fencing Federation[2] in 1906 to form the organisation which became today's French Fencing Federation.[3]

His book <u>Fencing through the Ages</u> is a view of the development of

---

1. *Société d'Encouragement de l'Escrime*
2. *Fédération nationale d'escrime*
3. *Fédération française d'escrime*

fencing which is informed by two major themes in nineteenth century and in French cultural thought. Corthey sees the history of fencing in France as the history of escaping the dominance of Italian culture and thought in order to develop a native French fencing. This conforms to a common saying that French culture has Italian roots and is based on the idea that the exporting of Italian humanism and literature during the fifteenth century filled a void as France emerged from the intellectual darkness of the Middle Ages. He highlights Henry de Sainct-Didier, whose text is the first known to be written in French, as the first step in this direction while at the same time recognizing it as a dead end. He discusses briefly more well known masters such as La Perche, L'Abbat, Liancourt, claiming Thibault as the grand master of rapier swordplay, before coming to the period in which French fencing comes into its own: the small sword and foil fencing of Besnard, Angelo and their contemporaries. The foil was a French invention as was the fencing mask. It is now that French fencing comes into its own and escapes Italy.

On the second theme, it is harder to know exactly where Corthey's opinion lies. The grand narrative of progress states that, due to the careful application of human reason, the art of combat, as all other arts and sciences, improves and refines itself over time. Fencing as combat began, he says, with hands and teeth when two people fell into disagreement. Medieval combat was more a matter of the blacksmith's skill in producing armour than the knight's skill with the sword. Only after the introduction to the battlefield of gunpowder weapons rendered medieval armour useless and combatants began to use the sword for both attack and defense was fencing in the true sense born. Incremental improvements ever after move the art inch by inch towards perfection. However, Corthey recognizes that this progress was not smooth but a matter of fits and starts. Fighting with a single handed sword progressed through several stages in which the sword was used for the attack while another tool (buckler, dagger, cloak, etc) served to defend before the innovation was hit upon to use the same weapon for defence that is used for attack.

In recognizing the uneven progress – though progress nonetheless – of the development of fencing, Corthey singles out certain periods for more in-depth attention. The first of these is the appearance as if out of nowhere of fencing with the two-handed sword, spadoni and zweihanders rather than longswords. This fencing is puzzling in its completeness and sophistication and more so when compared to the primitive fencing with the sword alone or sword and buckler which follow its equal mysterious disappearance.

The chief indicator of a fencing's location on the ladder of progress is the degree to which the sword both attacks and defends. Two-handed swords have this quality but are followed by more primitive styles of fencing using the sword solely to attack and some other object in the left hand to defend, such as the buckler, dagger, cloak, etc. Marozzo is the great examplar and teacher of combat with the single sword. Saint-Didier appears to him most primitive of all in that he uses the left hand to defend with nothing in it. It is only towards the end of the seventeenth century with the foil of Besnard and the small sword of the next century that perfection came within reach. It is only when gunpowder came to dominate the battlefield that fencing as something like the art he knew was born.

The Report gives a clear indication of Corthey's mind and how he approaches issues of historical fencing in the present day. Modern fencing, that is fencing with the foil, has become an almost "mathematical science" in which irresistible attacks may be executed in near perfect safety and parries may be made in close to absolute security. The contest has become one of skill, courage and mental acuity, no longer a test of mere athleticism. The skills and techniques of modern fence, with the inexorable certainty of progress, are used for sport and entertainment but cannot, however, be applied to the more serious business of honour and the duel. (It should be noted here that Corthey was a second in a duel that never eventuated and seems to have been fought solely in the letters columns of various newspapers.)

Corthey's genius is that he lays the fault not on the duellists and their instructors and teachers but on the shape of the weapon itself. The techniques, refined through the ages, that are applicable for a square cross-sectioned foil cannot be performed with a triangular bladed dueling épée. He spends most of the Report listing the deficiencies of this weapon before proposing an épée blade with the quadrilateral, if not rectangular, cross-section in order to bring the art of dueling into line with the science of fencing.

In this, he maintains perfect consistency of thought with the ideas he expresses in Fencing through the Ages.

*List of Works Cited*

Corthey is widely read and cites many books, both related to fencing and literature.

- Anon. The Matter of France, The Old Testament
- L'Abbat de Toulouse (Labat). The Art in Feats of Arms
- Alfieri, Francesco. *La Spadone*
- Angelo, Domenico. The School of Arms
- Besnard, Charles. The Master of Free Arms
- Bourdeille, Pierre de (Brantôme). Oeuvres Complètes

4   Fencing through the Ages

- Cervantes, Miguel. <u>Don Quixote</u>
- Colombey, Eduardo. <u>Anecdotal History of the Duel</u>
- Corneille, Pierre. <u>Horace</u>
- Cyrano de Bergerac, Savinien de. <u>The Comical History of the Moon and the Sun</u>
- Danet, Guillaume. <u>Treatise on the Art of Arms</u>
- Diderot, Denis. <u>The Grand Encyclopedia</u>
- Feval, Paul. <u>Le Bossu</u>
- Girard, Pierre Jacques François. <u>New Treatise</u>
- La Boëssière, Antoine Texier. <u>Treatise on the Art of Arms</u>
- Le Perche du Coudray, Jean-Baptiste. <u>The Exercise of Arms or the Handing of the Foil</u>.
- Moliere. <u>The Bourgeois Gentleman</u>, <u>Fourberies de Scapin</u>
- Machiavelli, Niccolo. <u>The Prince</u>
- Marozzo, Achille. <u>Opera Nova</u>
- Noirmont, Dunoyer de; Marbot, Alfred de. <u>Costumes militaires francais</u>
- Saint-Didier, Henry de. Traicte <u>Contentant les Secrets de l'Epee Seule</u>
- Scott, Walter. <u>The Constable of Chester</u>, <u>The Fair Maid of Perth</u>
- Thibault, Gerard. <u>Academy of the Sword</u>
- Vigeant, Arsene. <u>La bibliographie de l'escrime ancienne et moderne</u>

Other authors referenced without specific titles:

- Agrippa, Camillo
- Dumas, Alexandre
- Fabris, Salvatore
- di Grassi, Giacomo
- Latouche, Philibert
- Lebkommer, Hans
- Liancour, Andre de
- Zola, Emile

*The Text and Translation*

All texts translated in this volume are in the public domain and are used here on that basis. No infringement of copyright is intended.

These text presented here fall into two categories: those written by Corthey himself and those written by others about him or his works. Nothing of significance need be said about the latter category: the silhouette is a fairly ordinary piece of writing, the press reports on the various historical fencing displays are typical for French journalism and editorials of the period. About

Corthey's own writings, he uses a very direct style which makes for generally easy translation. Unsurprisingly, given his literary background, his works are full of allusions to stage and literature and his legal background perhaps accounts for the clarity of expression through which he makes his point.

The translation is literal where possible. Some liberties have been taken with tense, word order and sentence construction where a literal translation would be sufficiently unclear as to obscure the meaning of the text. Idiom has been replaced more modern expressions where the original does not translate cleanly. These are footnoted.

Parentheses () in the text are present in the original text as are untranslated words and phrases in italic type. Brackets [] are clarifications of mine which do not warrant a formal footnote.

# Adolphe Corthey

1834–1900

*These three extracts give an overview of a man committed to furthering both fencing as a sport and in earnest, and investigating the origins and development of the discipline. Corthey shows that the late nineteenth century interest in the history and historical practice of swordsmanship was just as keen in France as in Britain.*

*From: <u>Le Sport en France et à l'Étranger – Silhouettes Sportives</u>[1], Vaux,Charles-Maurice de, Paris, 1898, pp.233-236*

Who does not know Adolphe Corthey? There is not a good meeting of weapons without him and the clicking of foils attracts him — like the sound of cannon [attracts] the brave.

Born in Lausanne[2] in 1834, Corthey, who is 65 years old today,[3] is without contradiction one of our more remarkable foils. His vigour is extraordinary. He is a tall indeed, very solidly built, with big black eyes lighting up face energetic but full of kindness.

Activity is Corthey's characteristic.[4]

---

1. <u>Sport in France and Abroad - Sporting Profiles</u>
2. Switzerland
3. Date of reference 1898

At the age of nine years, he entered in a gymnasium and led from the front the education of character and of intelligence.

The progress which Corthey made was rapid; he had understood immediately that gymnastics was the start and the finish of all the exercises of sport.

When we saw the army of these audacious youth who frequent the gymnasiums of Paris throw themselves at the mats, suspend themselves by ropes and [who] swim in space, step to the vault on these lines to multiple inflexions, to leap, to clear in a bound these obstacles which frighten, then, after the struggle and the audacious aerialists of the trampoline, playing with weights, the barbells and the iron bars, to run in folding oneself, to dance like a gladiator of Rome, we understand that the body thus fashioned, twisted, pressed,[5] made supple, strengthened, finds itself admirably prepared for the varied applications of the sporting life.

At the same time that he worked gymnastics, Corthey exercised himself at shooting with the pistol at first, that of the carbine following, and finally that of the bow where he obtained several rewards including a first prize; nothing extraordinary for a compatriot of William Tell. The neighborhood of Léman led him to canoeing. In France we delight with a certain naivete in the widespread[6] and very deeply rooted prejudice against canoeing. We do not want to see canoeing, even for the son of the proletarian, in idleness, good at best for shaping loafers. The Swiss do not think this way.[7] They know too well from which side we can draw courageous men, skilful and strong; also she encourages with these sympathies all these young people who engage in this kind of sport. Canoeing in Switzerland is not a game, it is a serious occupation, a teaching which has its disciples, its rules and its incentives.

Since he had been familiarised with canoeing, Corthey, who wanted to practise all the sports, learned the fight, English and French boxing, fencing with foil and sabre, and horsemanship. He only neglected one single exercise, that of skating. I would dare not affirm but I well believe that his indifference for this sport comes from that it is in France a pastime[8] rather than an exercise. One can love to skate only there or where the climate allows for long walks on the ice, exploration of the countryside,[9] even journeying. The pleasure born

---

4. *la caractéristique de Corthey, c'est l'activité*
5. lit. broken, severed
6. lit: numerous
7. *la Suisse ne procède pas ainsi*
8. *un plaisir*
9. *villégiature*

of the extent and beyond the speed of racing; yet it is something to be able to, without fatigue, traverse space at the speed of a horse at the gallop.

After having achieved the sporting spectrum, Corthey limited himself to boxing and fencing, these are two sports that he practices daily, and in one or the other he passes for an extremely difficult opponent.

Vigour is not something Corthey lacks.[10] He has legs of iron which bend like springs, a hand of unforgettable lightness and the lungs of a racehorse. He shows always a very sure judgement and a remarkable timeliness.[11] He attacks and ripostes with equal superiority. He takes *contres* and *double-contres* of *sixte* and ripostes often by disengaging in the low line.

Not content to be a finished fencer,[12] Corthey is also a worker. It is to him we owe the creation of the historical bouts. That which he organised, some years ago at the Cirque d'Ete, amazed the world. He wrote several works on fencing, among others <u>The Foil and the Epee</u>, <u>A Treatise on Fencing with the Bayonet</u> and recently a volume on <u>Fencing through the Ages</u>.

We owe again to this sportsman the creation of the rectangular épée for the duel and the assault and a completely new bayonet[13] for replacing that of the Lebel rifle and, in collaboration with M. Gaston Andrieu, a cavalry sabre which will before long, we believe, be adopted by the army.

M. Corthey is one of the rare sportsmen who has no enemies; the loyalty of his character, his modesty, his profound knowledge of fencing are unanimously appreciated.

---

From: <u>Gil Blas</u> *(Paris) 30 October 1900, No.7652, A.21, p.4*

## The Death of M. Corthey

M. Ad. Corthey died yesterday at the age of 66 years in his apartment on the rue Lepic.

For a year, heart disease[14] distanced this gallant amateur from the *Ecole d'Escrime Francaise* where he practiced arms daily for long years, as well as at the *Salle Gabriel*.

Who has not known this charming talker, this erudite fencer, who refused no one a bout?

10. *la vigueur, ce n'est pas ce qui manque à Corthey*
11. *d'un à-propos remarquable*
12. *escrimeur complet*
13. *une baïonnette toute nouvelle*
14. *une maladie de coeur*

We have often spoken here of his books on old-time fencing and his incessant efforts which were in favour of the propagation of fencing.

The sabre takes currently to a great extent in France. We forget not that this weapon had M. Corthey as one of its fervent defenders.

Lawyer and writer, he often put his biting and spiritual pen in the service of arms.

He was a believer who joined practise to theory.

Everyday, he raised his fantastic weight, delivered a boxing or fencing bout. He had not lost an inch of his height and his vigorous pace was the best argument in favour of physical exercise.

We little expected that the sad news which propagated so rapidly yesterday in all the fencing salles and which caused there the deepest regrets because French fencing has lost in M. Corthey one of its dedicated representatives.

All the friends of the sword, all those who knew him from far or near, the elders as well as the young, will respectfully salute his memory.

*Willy Sulzbacher*

---

*From: La Presse (Paris) 31 October 1900, No.3077, p.3*

We regret to learn of the death of M. Adolphe Corthey, the well-known sportsman, swordsman doubling as a writer and most distinguished playwright. M. Adolphe Corthey wrote stories appreciated and represented on the stage in several acts in the style of Labiche which have achieved a deserved success. M. Corthey also devoted himself passionately to military issues.[15] He was in this capacity of the Military Press Union.[16]

Well-known in Parisian society where he had the most lively and most numerous sympathies, M. Corthey will leave unanimous regrets.

His funeral will take place tomorrow at 11:30. We will meet at the funeral home, 41 rue Lepic.

---

15. *questions militaires*
16. *Syndicat de la Press Militaire*

# Fencing through the Ages

by Adolphe Corthey
Preface by Henry de Goudourville
Paris
Charles Dupont, Editor
42 Rue de Trévise, 1892

---

**Works by the Same Author**

| | |
|---|---|
| Foil and Epee: a Study | 1 fr |
| French and Prussians: Sidearms and Firearms (second edition) | 1 fr |
| A Little Treatise on Fencing with the Bayonet (second edition) | 1 fr |
| Report on the Subject of the Transformation of the Combat Sword (second edition) | 1 fr |

For the Society for the Advancement of Fencing[1] and under the very distinguished president, Henry de Goudourville

---

1. *Société d'Encouragement de l'Escrime*

# Preface

> It is also useful for a master of arms to frequent artists in all genres. Increasing his knowledge like this, he will convince himself more and more that the arts all rest on the same principles and that they have, if I dare to explain myself thus, a degree of kinship between them.
>
> — La Boëssière[1] (<u>Treatise on the Art of Arms</u>, p. 18)

It is probable that no one before M. Ernest Molier[2] had yet had the idea of presenting old-time fencing in the form of vignettes.[3]

Several years ago, he charged his friend M. Corthey with doing the necessary research, assembling the materials and creating the plays.

And it was under Corthey's direction, aided by Messers Vavassaeur and Roulez, that the presentation of historical bouts took place in the Circus, today destroyed, on the Rue de Benouville.

The study hereafter is at once a summary of the preliminary work necessary for this presentation and a colorful and living representation of the vignettes presented.

First in 1894, and in 1895 following, the Society for the Advancement, whose president M. De Villeneuve is always on the lookout for things related to swordsmanship, reprised the idea of a session of historical fencing.

And this work, which was the result of the first bout,[4] served as the basis for the two later [bouts], one of which was given at the Grand Hotel and the other at the Cirque d'Été, achieving immense success.

One should add that a score of fencers, experts and amateurs in the beautiful art of arms, devoted themselves entirely to the enterprise.

They were rewarded for this by the applause of the crowd and the willing-

---

1. Antoine La Boëssière, a fencing master, wrote a study of fencing called <u>Traite de l'Art des Armes</u>. His father, Nicolas, invented the fencing mask in 1780 and was an influential member of the French Academy of Arms.

2. Ernest Molier ran a private circus, the Circus Molier on the Rue de Benouville, from 1880 until his death in 1933 and was known as a particularly skilled showman and equestrian. His annual charity gala attracted the brightest stars of Parisian high society. See "At the Cirque Molier" and "Clown's Report from the Circus Molier" later in this volume.

3. *tableaux vivants* - scenes acted out on stage or in performance

4. French uses *assaut* which does not make contextual sense translated as "assault" in English; "bout" seems a better choice

16  Fencing through the Ages

ness that one saw everywhere to reproduce these historical bouts in Belgium,[5] and in England, and in Switzerland and in the provinces.

Moreover, in the world of arms, one has not forgotten the actors of these sword contests which were run as true dramas and the names of Messers Saint Chérun, Andrieu, Bruno de Laborie, count d'Oyley, J. Joseph-Renaud, Lécuyer, Bottet, Weber-Halouin, Georges Bureau, Salusse, de Murat, count Collarini, Leon Tissier, Lustgarten, Sulzbacher, Moreau-Dalmont, Lucien Leclerc, Gabriel and Mme Gabriel remain entirely in the memories of most spectators.

But the published study will not only have the result of recalling to the memory those beauties, it may be useful for the amateur as well as for the teacher.

A summary of fencing in the past, across the ages, and which bears, not only vignettes taken from life, the same things that would double as an historical overview of weaponry and methods of fighting, was, I believe, a work worth attempting.

M. Corthey, of whom I am honoured to be a friend, has with his alert pen already written the history of the sword which immediately follows this introduction.

I admit that his magnificent work could have done without my modest contribution but, obstinate as befits someone of reason, I must give in and accept the task – very sweet and very agreeable – of putting a header to the subject already examined. That is to say, for the canvas painted by the elder, the younger had to make a frame for according to his view, his knowledge of arms. And I accepted thinking that by this study swordsmanship was served by spreading interest[6] in it.

The master of arms studies so little today, the profession is spent,[7] a lazy regiment of so many unlettered provosts and masters often unsuited to any understanding,[8] that I ask myself if fencing will endure, will continue, along with the other arts.

In the choice of a student, the master of arms should, as I have already had occasion to say, search for qualities other than perfect agility.

One has so many times proved that a machine more or less well constructed was only dangerous for the man who does not know how to use it

---

5. Referring to the session in which Alfred Hutton participated. See "Letter from Belgium" later in this volume.

6. *le goût* - lit: the taste

7. *est tant courue*

8. *inaptes souvent à toute conception*

that I would believe it abusing my readers to depict a fencer superiorly agile but absolutely deprived of reason fencing against a thinking being, knowing how to combine and to measure the tempo. It is without doubt this latter who would win.

And it is for all these reasons, having treated on the teaching of the sword, as to why this or that, that I believe that a concise study of the weapon, followed by a quick history of the strikes used by the ancients, will not pass unnoticed by the man of arms, amateur or instructor.

*Henry de Goudourville*

# I

Fencing, if one takes the word in a very general manner, dates from the days when two men disputed something, the beautiful Helen or a plate of lentils.

Fingernails, teeth, feet, fists and the head were assuredly the first arms. Certain unsavoury types[1] in our modern towns still operate like primitive man.

Rocks, sticks, clubs only came later. Yet they are an indicator of a certain civilisation. And the philosopher could judge a society much more surely based on the manner in which they fight each other than based on the manner in which they dress themselves.

The head-breaker[2] is, on this point, more instructive than the breeches. With regard to fencing with the sword in particular, even though the weapon is ancient, the art of using it is nearly as recent as the science of the piano.

One proud knight did not know more than another.[3] The sword was for them solely an instrument a little more handy than a lance but that is all. From the point of view of defence, they were content to shield themselves like ships at a breakwater.[4] More akin to the sea turtle than to the desert lion, it was for them only a matter of being capable of receiving strikes which do not harm too much.

And the greatest warrior was he on whom one could beat the hardest and for the longest time without result.

Ultimately, his skill was not worth that of his armourer, his bravery was a matter of good manufacturing and he wore his courage as a shirt.

It should be added that it was from Germany that this type of courage came that is worn on the back. Yet the suit of padded mail[5] had probably been worn for the first time by the Normans.

Also, Walter Scott in the <u>Constable of Chester</u> shows us knights of this nation mocked by Gallic infantry who, wearing a simple linen shirt, fought thus adversaries covered with a carapace of steel.

It should be admitted that this carapace rendered good service at times. At Bouvines, Philippe Auguste owed it his salvation: thrown down from his horse,

---

1. *rôdeurs de barrière*
2. *casse-tête*
3. *les preux chevaliers ne connaissent pas plus l'un que l'autre*
4. *éperon*
5. *le complet de mailles rembourré*

trampled, and transforming himself on the battlefield like Sancho in the Isle of Barataria,[6] he emerged without a scratch.

But at Sempach, it played the Duke of Austria and his barons a very poor turn.[7]

After the combat, some hundreds of them were collected by the Swiss, their conquerors.

They [the Swiss] had no trouble with this because they [the Austrians] were dead. Inverted on their backs, they could not raise themselves and remained thus in the full summer sun. They had died suffocated like huge beetles.

In parentheses, these incidents allow us to suppose that these heroes, so cautious, were less strong than the legend tells and that common folk[8] believe.

If one judges by the arms on exhibit in the Artillery Museum, the shoulders of our simple gymnasts are as powerful as those of these supposed giants. One should add that the Swiss of this period, like the Welsh, like the Scots of the Highlands (also mountain-dwellers), like the ancient Gauls, their ancestors and ours, fought with chests uncovered.

Chivalry was perhaps not on their knights' side. Be that as it may, the first cannon changed everything. Between cannonball and cuirass, the game is not equal.

And the nobles, already beaten at close-quarters by lightly dressed infantry, killed now at distance by infantry armed with arquebuses, renounced the value of their vulnerable anvils[9] and abandoned their scrap-iron as useless.

On the one hand, infantry regained its importance, lost since the heyday of Rome; on the other, single combats followed the fashion of pitched battles. Adversaries on foot began to defend themselves with attacking weapons.

And fencing was born.

In this manner, up to a certain point, one could say that it is the gun that made the sword.

---

6. Referring to Sancho Panza and an incident in <u>Don Quixote</u>
7. *un bien villain tour*
8. *le bon bourgeois*
9. *la qualité d'enclumes vulnérables*

# II

It seems to us today completely natural to defend ourselves with the same weapon which we use[1] to attack. Nevertheless this idea, which seems so simple to us, took several centuries to develop in our minds.

At first, it was hardly more than intuition.

This is the moment to speak of a curious weapon, gigantic and terrible, which appears suddenly, plays a considerable role, if one believes the first works on fencing, then disappears as it came, almost without leaving a trace.

It is the two-handed sword.

It is not, however, the sword itself which is unknown. One sees, on the contrary, beautiful specimens in the Artillery Museum, in nearly all the arsenals and in the houses of many antiquaries. That which seems completely forgotten is that there existed an art of how to use it.

So, in M. Molier's first session,[2] the bout which took place between Messers Jeannonet and Boudin, and which had been directed by M. Vavasseur, equally an amateur, produced a kind of bewilderment in the spectators.

Let us suppose that any animal trainer, Bidel or Pezon, dared to exhibit in his menagerie a megatherium or a living ichthyosaur and made them do their various exercises. The effect would be a little near the same.

In reality, where does this mastodon of fencing come from? The Greeks, the Romans, the Spanish[3] and later the Franks, made swords which were only heavy knives. On the other hand, we believe we know that certain peoples of Gaul used long broadswords which they were, it seems, forced to use two-handed.

If this information is correct, it would seem to demonstrate for the mountain-dwellers of the centre of Switzerland and the Scots of the Highlands a common origin since it is with these two peoples, nonetheless very far apart, that one finds in a relatively recent period the most frequent use of the large spadone.[4] And this would be the last trace, carefully preserved by these mountain-dwellers, of the weapon with which our ancestors the Gauls, after having crossed the Alps and crossed Europe, battered the Roman legions in Italy and cut to pieces the Macedonian phalanx at Delphi.

1. lit: serves us
2. See "At the Cirque Molier" and "A Clown's Report from the Circus Molier" in this volume
3. *Cantabres*
4. *espadon*

It should be added that the Swiss and Scots do not have the exclusive monopoly on the two-handed sword.

The broadsword of Jacques the Conqueror,[5] preserved in the Madrid museum, is one example of such. Rabelais makes mention of a sword of this type and Froissard cites an English knight who used one in the war about the time of Du Guesclin.[6]

That which is certain is that from the first fencing with this weapon is relatively sophisticated[7] and that the weapon itself is cleverly designed.

That the blade may be flat or fullered, or with stops[8] or lacework or flamberg, with the end sharp or rounded or larger than the base, nothing is given to chance.

And even though the hilt of the ordinary sword is barely more than a simple cross, that of the great sword is armed with defences, not only to protect the hands, but to allow the person to act effectively in an unlikely but possible body-to-body [encounter].

The authors who concern themselves especially with the two-handed sword, or at least speak of it, are half a dozen. In 1529 Lebkommer, a German; in 1536 Marozzo, an Italian; the anonymous writer to whom one owes the <u>Sword Player</u>[9] published in Anvers; Thibault; Alfieri.

This last, one would hardly believe it, is a contemporary of Molière and his treatise appeared very close to the moment when <u>The Bourgeois Gentleman</u> was performed.

It is probable nonetheless that the Dutch, Germans and Italians had to import the spadone from the Swiss, who had beaten the Austrians on Swiss territory, the Germans in Swabia, fought the Burgundians in the Pays de Vaud, the French and the Spanish in Italy. It is not doubted that, until the Burgundian wars, that is to say from the Battle of Mortgarten to that of Saint Jacques, it was for the Swiss the principle weapon with the halberd and the "morgenstern," a type of mace ending in a point and bristling with other points on its upper part, all three about the same length, around two metres.

But, from that moment, the confederated troops,[10] for the most part at least, adopted the great pike and, if one believes the regulations and the images

---

5. King of Aragon (1213-1276)

6. Either Bertrand Du Guesclin (1320 - 1380), Constable of France, or Olivier Du Guesclin (died c. 1400), his brother and a celebrity of the Hundred Years War

7. *aussi complet* - finished and lacking no important part

8. schilts?

9. <u>Joueur d'Épée</u>

10. ie: the Swiss

published in the work of Messers Noirmont and Marbot, <u>Military Costumes of France</u>, it was the Landsknechts, imitators and competitors of the Swiss, who inherited the great sword.

From the point of view of fencing, it is regrettable to not be able to mention any authentic duel with the spadone. Nonetheless, Walter Scott, whose stories are from history to make amends for so much history which is fable, let's say, described in <u>The Fair Maid of Perth</u>, and according to the chronicle of the 14th century, a type of judicial meeting with it alone more moving than all the duels of Bussy, of Chicot, and of d'Artagnan together. This is the matter of two clans, rivals and irreconcilable enemies, who obtain from the king of Scotland permission to end their quarrel in his presence, weapons in hand.

On the day specified, thirty champions presented themselves on each side, dagger at the side and great claymore[11] in the hands.

At the signal given by the king, who presides over the ceremony surrounded by the lords of the court and the people of the town of Perth, the champions of both sides arranged themselves in three lines, each man at several paces from his neighbour in order to allow all to use their weapons.

At a second signal, they threw themselves at each other, excited by the noise of trumpets and the claymore at the ready. The strikes delivered with these colossal weapons were so terrible that within several minutes of the melee, the ground was already covered with blood, the injured and the dead.

Several had been decapitated. There were heads split to the shoulders, three quarters detached from the chest. Some combatants who lost hands,[12] separated from the wrist as if by the blade of a scythe, attempted a supreme effort in order to use their daggers.

The two troops were diminished by half.

They separated themselves by common accord in order to regain their breath. Then, the survivors threw themselves at each other anew, the injured as well as all those who yet possessed enough strength to stand upright.

Finally, on one side there remained only five or six combatants, all injured and dripping with blood; on the other, one, the chief, and he is uninjured. He tries to defend himself still by isolating his adversaries, like Corneille's <u>Horace</u>, but, driven to the river which runs close by, surrounded on all sides, his claymore shattered, not wanting to surrender, no longer able to fight, he makes one last leap and throws himself into the current where he disappears to the cries of the people and the victors, unable to follow him.

---

11. "Claymore" is the word actually used in the text
12. *dont une main est tombée*

Thus ends the renewed combat of he of the Romans[13] against the Albans.

Only, it must be admitted that according to the chronicle recounted by the storyteller, Corneille's play seems to have been written for a girls' boarding school[14] and that the tragic climax is not on the side of the story's tragedy.

Leaving aside the history and the drama, the narratives and the inventions, let us come back to fencing. For the study of the two-handed sword, it is above all to Marozzo that one should turn. He is in this regard the most complete of the authors of the period, if not in fact the oldest.

In his remarkable work, <u>Opera Nova</u> (1536), fencing with the spadone takes up about a third of the book with images. The two other thirds are dedicated to the study of sword and buckler, sword and dagger, sword and cape, the handling of the pike, halberd, poleaxe [15] and the dagger alone.

The sword alone, as Saint-Didier will say later, holds here a relatively small place and the book provides only a very primitive fencing, reduced to one very limited guard, a medium guard, and a low guard a little like our prime, our second and our third today.

Fencing with the two-handed sword seems here, to the contrary, from the start complete, as we have already said. The normal posture is very close that of today's grand baton, the right foot forward, the hilt of the weapon close to the hip, the left hand touching the pommel, the right hand close by the hip and the point of the weapon at eye height.

Except the arms are almost always extended. We flex them more today. This extension of the arms characterises all Italian fencing from the beginning until our day.

The parries are very varied. One could even in certain cases fault them for too much refinement and unnecessary contortions; such as the *guardia di croce*, the *guardia di becaha cesa*, the *guardia di becha passa*.

All of these parries are intended to protect the head, the flanks and the legs. With the grand baton the entire body is easily covered. It is even easier with the great sword, with immense quillions which give the weapon the form of a cross and protect, by the sole fact of their dimensions, the hands and the arms of the fencer and by a very slight movement his chest and face. It goes without saying that if the sword parries are already easier than those of the grand baton, the strikes of the one will be even quicker that the strikes of the other, despite the greater lightness of the latter.

---

13. Referring to Horace, or Horatio as he is known in English, on the Bridge
14. *un pensionnat de demoiselles*
15. *pertuisane*

This is the sabre compared the cane.

That which one cannot overstate is, at this relatively early period, the superiority of this fencing over others.

Although the short sword serves only to attack, the great [sword] serves the attack and the defense, turn by turn, even though in the play with the former the parry is made with everything one could wish for other than with the weapon itself: with the left hand, with the dagger, with the cape, with the buckler, with leaps, passes, voltes, voids, escapes in all senses. The great sword parries by itself.

And if we wanted to bring modern terminology to the parries of the old-time authors we would find all those that we employ today from *prime* to *octave*.

In Alfieri's work, <u>La Spadone</u>, published in 1653, we meet even strikes thrown as in our fencing with the bayonet.

Thus one imagines that the sword, such as one sees in our museums, is nothing but a monument to the size and strength of our ancestors.

It would be however high time to wipe the slate clean of this common legend.[16]

Specifically, about the two-handed sword, let us see who carried it. Machiavelli, a contemporary of the battles of Novara, Marignan and Pavia, talks about the Swiss troops. And after having in his <u>The Prince</u> done justice to their courage, their discipline, their superiority over all other infantry, he added that they were composed of small men, dirty and ugly.

According to a chronicle cited by Messers Noirmont and Marbot in the <u>Military Costumes of France</u>, they were a sturdy and squat people.

Squat according to the chronicler, small according to the historian, one sees therefore that if the weapon is gigantic those who used it were anything but giants.

Be that as it may, and despite the role that it could have played at a given moment, we must admit that the two-handed sword is no more a weapon of the past than of the future. It is an anomalous weapon.

---

16. *cette légende bourgeoise*

# III

If we have lingered[1] on fencing with the great sword, it is because this fencing, which is the furthest from ours by date, is that which approaches closest [to ours] by the methods it employs – the weapon being, as we have said, at once offensive and defensive. In truth, it should be, since the two arms are occupied in holding it and that the body is no longer protected by a cuirass.

"One is forced to be honest," says the song. Here, the song and fencing are in accord.

Also we will not say that the art of using this little needle that we call the foil comes directly from the use of this colossal blade that the Italians named the spadone.

In reality, modern fencing developed slowly and by a series of successive transformations. It is claimed that the world was created in six days. Fencing took three centuries to cut its teeth.

The first metamorphosis is the sword and buckler. The Middle Ages is a return to barbarism; the Renaissance is a return to Greece and Rome. Fencing does not escape the law of the other arts.

No longer armored but still using two hands, each with a special role, one to hit, the other to protect. Thus, the contemporaries of Machiavelli hardly fought differently to the heroes of Homer.

One celebrated duel characterises this period.

It is that of Jarnac and Châtaignerie. The name Jarnac has passed from history into general usage. It has become a popular word in the bad sense of term and the noun has been transformed into an injurious adjective, certainly incorrectly. The account of Brantôme, nephew of Châtaignerie, is there in order to witness it. Not only does he not carry any true accusation against his uncle's adversary, but he concludes from the details he gives that if one of the combatants was culpable, it was not Jarnac. He [Jarnac] was skillful and prudent in his training and in the lists,[2] thus, in everything. And yet this skilfulness would make a fencer of three months in the salle smile today.

But it is a hundred wagered against one that if, in our day, a strongman from a large market battled in the street against a small well-dressed gentleman and that if the latter broke the leg of his adversary with one of those graceful

---

1. lit: stopped ourselves for a small duration
2. *en champ clos*

kicks, as terrible as unexpected, that one teaches us in the salles, the bulk of the audience would cry foul.

People in everything and everywhere willingly applaud brutal force.

They are less sympathetic to the skilled adept.

Coming back to Jarnac and Châtaignerie, these two great lords exercised themselves like simple pianists. Over a woman, it seems. The story is almost as if from the operetta.

Francis I had forbidden them from combat. The first thing that Henry II did on ascending the throne was to permit it.

It took place in grand ceremony, one can almost say like a great fete, like a type of tournament.

One may imagine the ancient Hippodrome the day of an extraordinary spectacle, the spectator's [in their] richest costumes since the king presides surrounded by his court and the two actors, having brought all their friends, several hundred in number.

The weapons of the adversaries were the sword and buckler. If one believes an engraving inserted in the beautiful work of M. Emile Mérignac and several other contemporary prints, they had in addition helmets and cuirasses.

Nothing can be suggested to the contrary since Brantôme, who gives some details on the weapons of the two champions, who indicates spare swords from Jarnac and who speaks of a type of iron brassard[3] attached to the left arm of the latter, says nothing more.

This brassard is an invention of Caizo, Jarnac's Italian master. The latter, still suffering from a shoulder injury, could more easily hold the arm extended and oppose with a parry of greater force[4] Châtaignerie's strikes.

When the king gives the combat signal, the two champions are both at distance since it goes without saying that they had not engaged swords as one would do in our day. The most passionate and most vigorous[5] propelled himself at the other, weapon high, with the intention of surprising and even routing him.

The latter[6] receives the shock covering himself with his buckler held firmly at the end of the extended arm and searches to strike the assailant with a thrust or a cut passing under the defensive arm.

The former, feeling himself too engaged, disengages by changing guard.

---

3. A type of rerebrace – armour for the upper arm
4. *opposer une plus grande force de parade*
5. ie: Châtaignerie
6. ie: Jarnac

Each of them, then, by passing to the right and left, forwards and backwards, searches to force his adversary to uncover himself.

The more vigorous profits from the opening in order to make an entry and attempt to wrestle.[7]

The weaker searches to evade the hold by a volte and to stop a redoublement attack by a thrust to the eye.

Both change posture every instant. Sometimes the feet come near, the body nearly straight and rigid as if one was an ancient column; sometimes twisted and convoluted as a vine branch, the legs seeming to bend under the weight.

Finally, Jarnac finds the favorable moment for placing the famous strike that Caizo, his teacher, taught him. He cuts Châtaignerie's hamstring who falls injured to the great astonishment of all.

The vanquished believed himself so sure of his victory that he died not as a result of his injuries but from the rage that his defeat caused him, since he tore at his bandages.

As the crowd is logical in all things, even in its language, it is probable to date to this period that we name the *coupe-jarret*, those whose job is cutting people's throat.[8]

As we have come to see, it is Brantôme who indicated for us the character and the weapons of the adversaries. Concerning their fencing, it was evidently that of Marozzo, about whom we have already spoken regarding the two-handed sword, because he was not only the main teacher of the period but perhaps one can say the only. And Caizo, the master of Jarnac, must have been Marozzo's disciple.

Still, he[9] leaves us a comprehensive work for the time, ornamented with numerous and very beautiful engravings where fencing with sword and buckler holds a large place.

One finds here several varieties of buckler in all forms and in all sizes, one not larger than the brim of a hat, others capable of covering a man's body entirely. Sometimes round, sometimes oval, sometimes taking the form of a half-folded corset; this is the *piccolo brocchino*; this is the *targa*.

Regarding the sword that Marozzo seems to use, it has two edges and is of heavy appearance. Its guard is uncomplicated, composed of two branches that with the handle form a cross. Outside of these branches and in the axis of the two edges of the blade are two rings.

---

7. *coup de lutte*
8. Cutthroats in English, obviously
9. ie: Marozzo

In the guard position, the body of the fencer is sometimes straight, sometimes leaning forward. And the left leg is more often than not behind the right leg.

The postures are very varied, even a little theatrical. And, not only they are continued in Marozzo's immediate successors, Agrippa, Fabris, di Grassi, but one can say that until a certain point they are perpetuated in Italian fencing. Those who have seen Baron San Malato can easily grasp the idea.

One hits with a thrust or a cut. One advances or one retreats passing one foot before or behind the other, but one does not lunge. On the other hand, the two arms remain always extended. This extension in the arms, at least in that which holds the sword, is preserved in Italy. It is logical, moreover, as long as the feint does not exist.

Finally, one circles around one's adversary looking to make him open or to catch him uncovered.

With regard to the parries, it is the buckler which does everything.

And yet, however small, it can only parry on one side: from right to left. It is almost always thus. However, one finds in Agrippa an engraving in which one of the combatants uses his large buckler in order to push from left to right the arms of his adversary and gain the shoulder in order to make an attack.[10]

One sees therefore that this is our exercises in the cane, sabre and English boxing which most resembles this primitive fencing.

One even infers from it the turns of the arms, the hips and the head, since if Marozzo does not demonstrate them positively for the sword, he teaches them for the dagger.

Also, this explains the Jarnac's iron brassard. And it is not without intent, obviously, that Brantôme speaks of the bodily strength of his uncle.

If the fight today is a type of fencing with flat hands, fencing then was a fight with armed fists.

---

10. *pour faire une entrée*

# IV

France, in fencing as in the other arts, has continued for a long time to free its originality from foreign influence.[1]

Italy is everywhere her teacher and she submits to men as well as to ideas. At a given moment, everyone is Italian in France.

The teachers of fencing are Florentine or Venetian or Sicilian, just as are the sculptors, goldsmiths, chemists and alchemists, doctors, singers, comedians and diplomats.

Except, the student finishes by leaving the master behind.

This does not happen in a day.

Thus under Charles IX, Saint Didier wrote a work of fencing, <u>Traicte de l'Epee Seule</u> (1573). But this work, whose principal originality consists in teaching the sword without the dagger or any other weapons, whether offensive or defensive, seems not to have exercised any great influence on contemporary duellists because, until the reign of Cardinal Richelieu, one continues to fight with the sword in one hand and the dagger in the other.

The buckler was a sure defense before an adversary but it was an inconvenient utensil for walking in the streets or presenting oneself at court.

And, alone, the Scots of the Highlands who, like the Gauls their predecessors probably never had other armour, preserved bucklers, on the other hand, almost until our day.

Jarnac and Châtaignerie had not therefore, at least in France, many emulators or successors.

However, the left-hand dagger, which serves sword fighters during a certain period, is a leftover from the buckler.

It is composed of a pointed blade, ordinarily without an edge, and the bridge of the hilt is furnished with a long and large plate of steel.

Let us suppose a Scottish buckler whose disk is shrunk and the point lengthened; thus, the *main gauche*.

It would not be a very easy instrument to wear on the belt[2] so it is promptly replaced by the dagger composed of a sharp blade and generally with two edges furnished with a simple cross acting as a guard.

It is with this weapon that Bussy, du Gast, Vitteaux, La Garde, Antraguet

---

1. *est restée longtemps pour dégager*
2. *ce ne devait pas être non plus un instrument très aisé porter à la ceinture*

and other great lords and cutthroats who thrived until the end of the reign of Henry IV defended themselves – without speaking of the Messieurs les Mignons of Henry III[3] who while wearing corsets like women drew the sword as professional swordsmen.

Therefore, if we would understand French fencing, we should look again at the Italian masters.

We explained that the work of Saint Didier did not have much influence. His sword alone is not more "skilled" than that of the followers of Italy[4] and he deprived them of the dagger.

According to him, as according to them, the sword is only intended to hit and it is always the left hand which parries except that the left hand is unarmed and could not, in any case by consequence, furnish a riposte.

One sees immediately the inferiority of the play.

Moreover, in his work, as erudite as interesting, The Bibliography of Fencing, M. Vigeant notes that Saint Didier took for his guide the work of di Grassi, a work inferior to those of Agrippa and of Fabris.

Some examples will immediately[5] give an idea of his play. He brings together two fencers whom he calls one the Lieutenant, the other the Provost.

Thus on guard, the left foot forward, the sword extended at the height of the shoulder, the head and the body inclined in the direction of the adversary, the left hand held at the level of the ear.

The first strike of the Lieutenant is a cutting strike to the hamstring. He begins where Jarnac ended.

If the adversary parried or rather evaded the strike and if he [the Provost] strikes in his turn, the Lieutenant looks to prevent him hitting the arm with a reverse cut of his sword. If this reverse is again evaded and finds itself followed by a new strike, he [the Lieutenant] threatens the point at the Provost's eye, making a pass to the side or a half-turn.

Piercing the adversary's eye seems to be a technique favoured by several generations of fencers.

Thibault himself comes back to it several times and this famous strike, from which the drama *Bossu* draws a part of its success and which kills unerringly throughout five great acts, is perhaps less fantasy than one had supposed.

Set under Louis XV, the thrust of Nevers[6] is most simply a thrust which delays.

---

3. The Dainty Ones, Les Mignons, favourites of the king from 1574 to 1589
4. *que celle de ses émules d'Italie*
5. *sur-le-champ*
6. The Duc de Nevers is a character in the drama

Let us return to Saint Didier.

From passes by volte, hitting with a thrust and with a cut, stopping as often with the edge as with the point, the weapon sometimes at the height of the head, sometimes at that of the shoulder, sometimes lower than the flank, and the left hand following the motions of the right, he finishes with the seizure of the sword. After a type of man-on-man,[7] he grabs the guard of the adversary's weapon with the left hand.

This strike, which one may not call precisely delicate, was not nonetheless without danger. One must not forget that the blades of this period cut from both sides.

In practicing it today, one would probably earn one or two months of prison and several hundred francs in fines. Formerly, one could lose two or three fingers.

It is noted that this method of Saint Didier's still primitive school is repeated again in the quite perfected fencing of Angelo in 1763, after having traversed without difficulty four reigns and several interregna.

Be that as it may, it seems to us established that Saint Didier remains if not in a state of misunderstood genius at least of an isolated talent.

The school of Agrippa and Fabris keeps its dominance in France as elsewhere.

And the defeat of Quélus by Antraguet[8] was not of a nature to highlight the <u>Treatise of the Sword Alone</u>.

We know that in the famous meeting of the Mignons and the Angevins, Quélus had forgotten or lost his dagger and that he was riddled with strikes by Antraguet, who did not balk at using his own.

Quélus died after a month of agony.

Alexandre Dumas in dramatising this account has put it certainly at the centre but the elements had been furnished him by Brantôme and by L'Estoile.

That which is certain is that one of the Angevins and both of the Mignons, Maugiron and Schomberg, were killed with a cut. Antraguet, lord of Entragues, alone remained without injury.

The masters then, Italian and French, had not yet raised the scratch[9] to the heights of a principle.

The thrusting teachers[10] had not been born.

Thus, on the contrary, bloody duels[11] were not rare and Brantôme cites

---

7. *corps-à-corps*
8. Champions of the protestant-leaning Henry III and the ultra-conservative catholic Duc de Guise
9. *l'egratignure*
10. *les professeurs picotins*

several. In his <u>Anecdotal History of the Duel</u>, M. Colombey recounts that two swordsmen, who had no other reason to detest each other than that of being, each on his side, the terror of his entourage, met one day by accident.

On seeing each other, their first movement was to draw their sword and dagger, the second to put themselves in guard.

The combat did not last long. After three minutes, one of the adversaries had three sword cuts across the body. He should have fallen. He threw himself at the throat of his adversary, threw him to the ground with wrestling, on the ground filled him with dagger strikes. The buttonholes on his vest were increased to double, the chronicle says. One of these enraged was precisely the La Garde that we named earlier.

The most curious [part] of the affair is that no one died, neither one nor the other.

The duel of Count Montmorency, which was a meeting of three against three, is the last celebrated affair where the dagger played its part. The axe also played at its heart because the Count was executed by the order of Cardinal Richelieu. The grand man of state had found a very ingenious means of killing the duel ... decapitating the duellists.

Cyrano de Bergerac also was one of the most militant swordsman of this sword fighting[12] period. He had a quick wit. He is the author of <u>The Comical History of the Moon and the Sun</u> and Molière did not disdain from relieving him of several scenes to the benefit of <u>Fourberies de Scapin</u>. But he had a hand yet more active than the mind. Further, he had one of those noses which today would make a fortune in a theatre and which was his misfortune – and that of passers-by above all. Because after one of them seemed to look too attentively at this nasal appendage, he was immediately forced to draw the sword. Despite the care that one put into avoiding the mortal nose, it wasted no time in becoming the most deadly of organs.

In our period, where the language of political men is confused with that of market women,[13] we have less irritable noses.

We have summarised in a few lines fencing the sword with the buckler. We will pause still less on that of the dagger and of the sword.

Even if one of the weapons is changed, the methods are not. One sole modification is detectable. The sword, which has always been an offensive weapon, has not yet become a defensive weapon. One the other hand, the

---

11. *les duels boucheries*
12. *brettailleuse*
13. *dames de la halle*

buckler which had naturally not ceased to be a defensive weapon has become offensive in transforming itself into the dagger.

That is to say that the latter,[14] which ordinarily forms the parry, furnishes sometimes the riposte.

Moreover, this parry is much more varied than that of the buckler. It acts following the need, sometimes on the inside, sometimes on the outside, from above downwards and from below upwards, and even with the little quillons which form the cross.

It goes without saying that the dagger is held in the same manner as the sword, whose movements it accompanies. It is only in the depiction of tragedies that one looks to hit downwards from above, as if one were to give a punch on the Turk's Head[15] at the fair.

The postures of the play of the dagger with the sword are nothing new. They are only in general still more convoluted and more theatrical than those of the fight of the sword and buckler. Yet if the right hand finds itself often behind and at the height of the head, the two hands fall from time to time to the level of the ground.

One does not yet lunge. It goes without saying for example one continues to use passes, voltes and blocks.[16]

One can not know therefore enough to it repeat. The art of fencing, such as we understand it today, dates almost from yesterday. It dates from the discovery of this foil that we would like to outlaw today.

Until the reign of Louis XIV, the sword, the noble sword, this weapon that one is proud to have at one's side, limits itself to stabbing,[17] to cutting or slicing.[18] That which is called Durandal[19] or Joyous,[20] which belongs to Roland, to Bayard or even to Bussy d'Amboise is not greatly superior to the instrument of the pork butcher.[21]

---

14. ie: the dagger
15. Referring to the fairground strongman game, popular in 19th century markets, of smacking a hammer on a button to propel a weight up a pole to ring a bell
16. *coups d'arrets*
17. *piquer*
18. *a couper ou a decouper*
19. The sword belonging to Roland, Charlemagne's paladin in The Matter of France
20. The legendary sword of Charlemagne used to crown the kings of France until 1824
21. *charcutier* - perhaps delicatessen captures the sense better

# V

It is only from Thibault (1628) that the dominance of Italian fencing ceases in France.

Thibault is an innovator. Thibault is a scholar. Thibault would like to be the geometer of fencing.

That which is certain is that his work is enormous. <u>The Academy of the Sword</u>, a huge folio very artistic, moreover, with engravings and prints, is a true monument. For example, this monument makes one think of the Place de la Concorde yet despite the numerous explanations of the author, or perhaps because of the too numerous explanations, it is not always easy to untangle that which he wants to say.

The work begins with a type of anatomical plate giving the proportions of each of the parts and members of the body compared to the others. Then the author passes from anatomy to mathematics. And, taking as a single measure[1] the blade of the sword, he traces a large circle, in the circle numerous lines and on the lines he writes the letters which he will use to indicate the various positions of the legs of the fencers. And even as Saint Didier had his Lieutenant and his Provost who attack and parry turn by turn, Thibault chooses two adversaries to whom he gives the their own names, one being quite strange, Zacchary.

We will not try to analyze even by the table of contents Thibault's work despite its importance. In order to summarise this huge volume it would require at least a small [one].

What we can indicate is that which separates it from previous works.

For the first time, we find a teacher who indicates the means of parrying with the same weapon with which he attacked.

We do not include,[2] naturally, the two-handed sword.

One should add that the manner of this parry is not yet ours and can be only employed with the particular form of the sword of this period which is the sword called Spanish,[3] that is to say, a long blade provided with branches of large dimension and a complicated guard and counterguard.

It is in taking the opposing blade between his own blade and one of the quillions that Thibault forms the parry.

If the strike is thrown above, the sword will be lifted further as by a type

---

1. *pour unité de mesure*
2. *nous ne tenons pas compte, bien entendu* - we do not take into account
3. *espagnole*

of lever; if it is thrown below, in *cavation*[4] it will be further lowered in a similar fashion. In one case or the other, it will be brought back to the body.

Needless to add that for this type of work a supreme lightness of hand is not the custom.

This should not be too difficult for a period very close to the day where everything finishes not with song but with fighting.

Thibault has pretensions not only scientific but artistic since according to his lessons the adversaries, falling into guard, execute a type of preliminary movement which comes close to our salute.

One must admit that the position of the guard is not the most graceful, the body is nearly straight, the legs a little apart and the left arm hangs along the body. But it differs noticeably from that of the Italian masters.

On the other hand, fencers do not yet know how to lunge and in this respect they do hardly better than their predecessors. They engage in most of the usual movements, volteing, passing, mixing together thrusts and the cuts.

Except Thibault believes he can regulate with precision each of these movements and it is here that he triumphs with his circle, his lines and his alphabet.

This does not prevent him, in the last part of his book, from teaching [how] to fight with all offensive and defensive weapons: dagger, cloak, spear, shield, spadone and musket with the sword alone.

These lessons, a little fantastic, that most authors relegate to the last pages of their books, we will find again in the 18th century with Angelo, who further adds to these types of combat that of the dark lantern.

In order to see fencing almost approach that which it is today, one must come to the century of Louis XIV with Besnard, Latouche, Liancourt and Labat. Fencing, we see, is no exception to the world[5] of the other arts.

Besnard, whose work is less luxurious than those of Latouche and Liancourt, is perhaps more original. Firstly, it is the earliest by date. But all have common principles.

It is curious to note in this regard that progress, in fencing as elsewhere, is not made by a continual and upwards movement but by a series of actions, reactions and upheavals. Saint Didier had adopted the squashed guard[6] of the Italians; Thibault preferred[7] an almost upright stance; the masters of the century

---

4. The text has *cavation* in italics indicating that it is a foreign (presumably Italian) word. I assume it refers to a *cavazione* in period Italian fencing

5. *au milieu*

6. *la garde écrasée*

7. *patronise*

of Louis XIV returned to the squashed guard, only in place of having the body inclined forward, like the teacher of Charles IX, they placed it to the rear, on the very bent left leg. The right leg is thus quite extended forward.

Regarding the left arm, it is now placed behind and the elbow is in a slightly angular position.

The sword also is in contrast with that of the preceding generation.[8] The former is unmeasurably long; the latter is remarkably short, both [are] equally sharp on both sides.

We see all this in one engraving in the work of Latouche. This engraving which makes a pretty picture of the type of Poussin's style represents a bout at Versailles in the presence of the king.

What is striking is the prodigious lunge of the fencers. A reaction again, if one wants, but certainly an innovation. This is the true key to the French method.

In order to reach further, not only does one completely extend the left leg, one will even twist the foot on the inside in the manner that one can see the entire sole of the foot.

These teachers of the grand century are truly innovators, since one finds also in their teaching the riposte and the *contres*. With regard to this last, they recommend not to use them, it is true, at least in all serious occasions. They seem to see their utility only as an exercise.

We should not be astonished if they judge the simple parries incomparably more rapid. It is that the blade of the sword continues to cut from both sides. Yet, all fencers know the difficulty that there is to take a counter with a flat blade.

The *estramaçon*[9] has diminished in importance but it is not completely put to one side. It is the same for parries with the hand.

The left hand no longer parries by itself, but in certain cases, it comes to the aid of the sword by an opposition. We find this method again in La Boëssière, and it is only according to this last that the fanciful strikes disappear completely.

Thus the famous *Botte du Paysan*,[10] which consists using the sword with two hands, is from the XVII century. One should add that neither Besnard nor his successors attach importance to it any longer. The thrust of Nevers and

---

8. The text has *prédente* but I suspect this is an error and *précedente* is intended

9. Better known in Italian rapier fencing circles as the *strammazzone* - a quick, circular cut from the wrist

10. The Peasant's Thrust from La Touche in which the single handed sword is held with the left hand on the blade to break into the opponent's guard and thrust

that of the peasant, though not the same, make a pair. They, together, are also secrets.[11]

Apart from these particular authors, we have other documents, as M. Zola said.

We meet in the repertoire of one named Molière, who had thought to invent naturalism in order to avoid the natural, a certain play called <u>The Bourgeois Gentleman</u> in which one sees a certain scene which could well have been transported directly from the salle of Besnard to that of the king's theatre.

Here is this scene:

Act II. Scene III

*The master of arms, the master of dance, the master of music, M. Jourdain. The master of arms, who has taken two foils from the hand of a lackey.*

Come, Monsieur, salute. Your body straight, a little inclined on your left thigh. The legs spread thus far. Your feet on the same line. Your hilt held opposite your hip.

The point face-to-face with your shoulder. The right arm not at all so extended. The left hand at the height of the eye. The left shoulder more quartered. The head straight; the gaze assured. Advance. Body firm. Touch my sword in *quarte* and dominate the same. One, two. Return. Redouble with a firm foot. A leap backwards. When you carry the thrust, monsieur, the sword should speak first and the body should be covered. One, two.

Let's go. Touch my sword in *tierce* and dominate the same. Advance. Body firm. Advance. From there. One, two. Return. Redouble. A leap backwards. On guard, monsieur, on guard.

One will remark the term foil used by Molière. If we are not mistaken, it is the masters of the period of Louis XIV who used it first.

One will remark also the position that the teacher has put M. Jourdain into. It is scrupulously exact. This low guard is certainly borrowed from the work that Besnard published in 1653, well before the performance of Molière's play.

Moreover, the type of author of <u>The Master of Free Arms</u> should sue[12] the author of <u>The Bourgeois Gentleman</u>.

One can imagine it by the diatribe which ends the first's book. This dia-

---

11. *Elles sont aussi secretes, l'une que l'autre*

12. The word in the text is *tenter* (try, attempt) but the meaning is clear in context

tribe concerns pistol duels. Besnard does not content himself with sending the pistol to the devil, it is the devil who invented it.

By what circumstance is it not worn today, seeing that the weapon was particularly favored as the choice of the Deputies?[13]

But customs have softened. Perhaps he could content himself to note that the article of the law that the honourable still know best is borrowed from that of Moses.[14]

---

13. The Deputies of the French Revolution?
14. ie: the Law of Moses from the Old Testament, an eye for an eye, a tooth for a tooth

# VI

As much as the end of the 17th century is fertile in all things, the start of the 18th century seems hit with sterility by all reports.

Louis XIV has aged. He has become devout. He has slipped through[1] the hands of his confessor and into the arms of an old mistress. The people vegetate in the interior and armies battle in the exterior. All seem to feel this situation uneasy and sad: in the theatre as well as literature, swordsmanship as well as the arts.

Between <u>The Art in Feats of Arms</u> of Labat (1690)[2] and <u>The School of Arms</u> of Angelo (1763) we have nothing if not for the <u>New Treatise</u> of Giraud.

However, if fencing remained stationary, it did fall into decadence.

The body of the fencer has now acquired a withdrawn position. One precedes the bout with a salute. One lunges. One ripostes. Leaps, voltés, passes, blocks are no more than an exception. One fences in place.

Already the word foil, if not the thing we understand today, has been in circulation for a long time. Besnard is one of the first to name it. We have found it already in the play of <u>The Bourgeois Gentleman</u> in 1670, and Le Perche in 1676 entitled his treatise <u>The Exercise of Arms or the Handing of the Foil</u>.

Dating from 1763, a group of amateurs and teachers, the five stars of fencing, form a sort of constellation: they are Angelo, Danet, La Boëssière junior, the Knight of Eon, Saint-Georges.

Angelo is an Italian who wrote in England according to the French principles. His work is certainly the most luxurious and the most artistic of all the fencing treatises along with that of Thibault.

One could even without exaggeration call them together princely, since the authors had great lords and kings for collaborators, if not from the point of view of the pen at least from that of money.

Danet, for his <u>Art of Arms</u>, had not the honour to be patronized by sovereigns.

Far from that, he was treated as revolutionary by the Academy of Arms of Paris, who, through the intermediary of La Boëssière senior, reproached him for his audacious principles.

Academies, in general, will only voluntarily admit new men when they are old.

---

1. lit: fallen between
2. Actually 1696. A book, <u>The Art of the Sword</u>, was published in 1690 attributed to Labat.

Even so, La Boëssière invented the grilled mask. This quality of inventorship should have made him indulgent towards the innovator.

About the mask, one will remark on what pains we had in order to have it accepted.

"Good for clumsy boors," said the teachers of the period.

The mask, for which Angelo gives the design in his book, resembles less that which we use today than that with which children cover their faces at carnival time.

Danet was avenged, the father by the son. The former had attacked his[3] principles in a pamphlet, the second borrowed some of them from him in his <u>Treatise on the Art of Arms</u>.

And this <u>Treatise on the Art of Arms</u>, which dates back around 80 years, remains still the first of all. Some contemporary teachers can flatter themselves with having perfected certain details but many of them show too often that they have ignored the whole.

Regarding this strange personality who is named the Knight of Eon,[4] and whom we wanted to surname the Joan of Arc of fencing because she made assaults in petticoats, was man but, one should add, only with other men.

By turns, a diplomat in Russia, captain of dragons in France, and a demoiselle in England, she used certain natural features in order to play her century as effectively as her foil.

Be that as it may, man-woman or woman-man, with or without petticoats, the Knight or Dame[5] of Eon was certainly a remarkable fencer because he or she defended himself [or herself] against Saint Georges.

Yet, without holding the legend to account, one would be wrong to believe that this latter had been overrated.

The son of a grand French lord and a black woman, a mulatto by consequence like Jean-Louis,[6] and like the grandfather of M. Alexandre Dumas, he was tall, svelte and at once strong like the Marshall of Saxony and agile like a clown.

Further, gifted by nature with an active mind and a hot imagination, his master had given him composure[7] by making him work five hours a day.

---

3. ie: Angelo's

4. Charles-Geneviève-Louis-Auguste-André-Timothée d'Éon de Beaumont (5 October 1728 – 21 May 1810): a French diplomat and spy known for his androgynous features who infiltrated the Russian court as a woman and later lived solely as a woman. The gender of the pronouns used in the text are preserved in the translation.

5. *le chevalier ou chevalière*

6. La Boëssière's continuer - see below

The La Boëssières were marked for greatness,[8] since if the son made the best fencing treatise that exists, the father made Saint-Georges, that is to say, the best fencer known.

Also, in order to combat, even with disadvantage, this man at once fox and lion, one needs one other phenomenon.

One engraving of the time shows us the bout which took place in London in presence of the Prince of Wales between the Dame of Eon and the Knight of Saint-Georges.

In the first image, the two adversaries, heads bare, masks to the side, fence the wall. The Dame lunges and is even very extended; the Knight is nearly upright, the body a little behind, resting on the left leg, slightly bent. Both the postures are elegant.

Regarding the strikes that the fencers will make, regarding the parries that they will use, it is not difficult to make an account of them, since Eon had been Angelo's collaborator in the composition of his treatise.

Of the general method, one can say that the strikes will be at once cautious and fast, and that they will be thrown in all lines turn by turn; that the parries will be varied, sometimes composed of *simples*, sometimes of *contres*, always followed by the riposte.

The two champions explored each other at first certainly; they do not want to give anything to chance. They made false attacks. They threw half-thrusts and the feints which will follow these preliminaries will have all the subtlety that we could give them today. These will be the one-two, the counter-disengagements, the false attacks.[9]

The ripostes will not be only direct, in third as in fourth, in prime as in second, they will be from circles, from strikes and from half-circles.

The parries will be necessarily even more varied than they are today, because the body, less bent than it is now, exposes further the low line.

Finally, parries and ripostes, feints and attacks, will be made in place; barely will the opponents use by chance or as a last resort the demi-volte or evasion[10] of the left foot, this strike that the late Pons the Nephew[11] placed with such mastery.

From this bout, one can deduce several consequences. The first is that in the period of Angelo, the position of the guard is no longer the same as accord-

---

7. *le sang-froid*
8. The word used is *prédestinés*, but the sense is clear in context
9. *des trompés d'engagements*
10. *échappement*
11. presumably Charles Pons (1793-1885), fencing master to Napoleon III

ing to the masters contemporary with Louis XIV. The body is still carried on the left leg but the fencer is more withdrawn.

The right hand is place higher, the left hand also. Moreover, the arm is rounded further but the bend is less exaggerated. Finally, the attacks are only made to the torso and they are exclusively composed of strikes with the point. However, the foil still has a flat blade. It retains this form at least until the moment where it seems Diderot's The Grand Encyclopedia gives it a definition.

Further, Angelo speaks in several places of the inside and outside of the blade.

One explains thus why everyone does not reject the counter parries in the bout, as did the masters of the previous century. He prefers however to use simple parries.

It is only with La Boëssière junior that we find ourselves fully into the modern science.

We do not want to insinuate that there is nothing more to add to his lessons but we can affirm that there would be benefit to meditating on the them often. Since if the strikes of finesse and delicateness that we practice today were found largely developed in the treatise of La Boëssière, we have neglected a little those to which he attaches such importance, those of precaution[12] and of precision.

According to this teacher, in effect, attacks, like ripostes, are made without abandoning the steel with a type of rotation of the hilt, a powerful opposition and a huge elevation of the hand.

One could say that up to a certain point each of these movements holds simultaneously the *time* and the *line*; although these two types of strike seem at first mutually exclusive.[13]

Thus, with the system of La Boëssière the strike-for-strike is in a manner of speaking impossible, at least very difficult.

Today, we seem to preoccupy ourselves only with speed, that which is at its root the negation of the science.

With La Boëssière, speed alone will only serve to get you hit faster.

He explains his thoughts well when he says that "it is the foil of the adversary which must serve to guide yours." Joining therefore in his system the greatest security to the most extreme finesse, one must not be astonished that he had carried the art of fencing to its culminating point.

---

12. *sûreté*
13. *semblant au premier abord s'exclure*

Jean-Louis, his continuer, has shown by example that which is valued by the theory.

One knows this duel, absolutely incomparable, in which a terrifying fencer, then master of arms of a French training regiment in a Spanish village, battled with thirteen Italian masters and killed or injured successively his thirteen adversaries in the presence of all the troop and of all the village,[14] who attended solemnly this meeting, like a new judgement from God or … a battle of bulls.

In order to recount the exploits, as true as improbable, of this grand-son of d'Artagnan, M. Vigeant seems to have borrowed the pen of Dumas senior.

Yet that which characterises the system of La Boëssière is the position of the body and the legs.

We have seen that, according to Saint Didier, the latter were very bent and the former was very inclined forward; according to Thibault the body and legs are nearly straight; according to the masters of the 17th century the body is withdrawn over the left leg; according to those of the 18th century it rises again but is again inclined backwards; according to La Boëssière alone is it seated on the two legs equally.

Further, according to him, the use of the square foil is indisputable but it is difficult to confirm the exact moment when it made its appearance.

One could assume that the moment is, as we have already said, after 1763.

And it is precisely the use of the square foil which allowed La Boëssière to give his art the last refinements.

One feel strongly that[15] if the *contres* can be made with a speed nearly equal to that of the simple parries, it is only with the square blade. Also, we have seen the masters of the 17th century, all knowing perfectly the first, abandon them for the second.

Therefore, we cannot protest too strongly against the use of the triangular blade.[16] Created from an idea, patronised by routine, bad for combat where they cannot hit with a cut, bad for the assault where they only provide for inadequate parries, as without finesse as toothless, their use in the duel has no other purpose because we have never asked for one.

Also, we would like to see the replacement of the triangular blade by the square blade with four fullers.[17]

---

14. *la population*

15. *On ne songe pas assez que*

16. See the Report of the Committee of the Society for the Advancement of Fencing On the Subject of the Transformation of the Combat Sword in this volume

17. *la lame carrée à quatre évidements*

The new weapon would preserve thus the advantages of the foil without having the inconvenience of the épée.

That which one should finally note according to La Boëssière is the care given to the parry.

It should not be forgotten, moreover, that all the grandmasters since Agrippa have always put defence well above attack.

And it is perhaps because that in our days one has often taken the exact opposite[18] of this theory that swordplay has come to grow on the back of fencing like a type of lump.[19]

The classical art evaporated into the fantasy of the self-styled science[20] of the duel, which is in reality only a return to primitive times, is at the same time also a memory of good sense.

And if it is necessary point out this trend towards decay, one knows not to blame any longer the teachers who seem to have carved on their bouting sword this device borrowed from the servants of private offices: "caution and discretion."

The end

18. *contre-pied*
19. *gibbosité*
20. *la prétendue science*

# Press Reports

*Four reports from the contemporary press are included here to demonstrate the manner in which the displays of historical or period fencing alluded to in* Fencing through the Ages *were received.*

*The first two refer to the first session held at the* Circus Molier *in 1887 as part of the annual circus gala solely for entertainment value rather than as an activity associated with the Society for the Advancement of Fencing for demonstration or educational purposes.*

*The third is one of the re-created and repeated sessions staged by the Society itself at the Grand Hotel, Paris in 1894. This is the session referred to in the fourth translated clipping which details an event put on the* Cercle d'Escrime of Brussel *in 1894, to which Alfred Hutton and his group from the London Rifle Brigade were invited.*

# At the Circus Molier

*Le Monde Illustre*, 18 June 1887, p403

The two annual evenings offered by M. Molier to certain happy privileged constitutes one of the most elegant meetings of Parisian high society[1] who amuse themselves and the presentations of the circus, so charmingly set in the courtyard of the small hotel in the Rue de Benouville, are always one of the most sought out attractions which can be seen.

There is nothing quaint or original as far as this stage, framed in decoration including the balconies of Spanish houses or the galleries of Moorish palaces, on which piled the crowd of the invited.

The program for this year was one of the best combined and numerous surprises were arranged.

Our illustration summarises some of the more curious exercises and most entertaining numbers.

Among the artists of the elite troop that the director of this exceptional circus has grouped together, our friend and collaborator M. Adrien Marie welcomed a large share of the applause with the tour-de-force that he accomplished. He painted on a horse at the gallop a picture whose rapid execution surprised all attendees who greatly admired[2] this very spiritual fantasy executed by the amiable painter. We cite again the belly dancing[3] by the gracious Mlle Rivolta; the entry of the clowns by Mme Dezoder from the Palais-Royal, of Brieges and Menty; the stunning work of M. H. de la Rochefoucald whose suppleness equals that of the most celebrated professional gymnast; the jumping horse of Mlle d'Yvrès of the elite school by Mlle Valberg; the strength exercises of M. Van Huisen, a sportsman who playfully lifts weights of 170 kg; and finally the remarkable horse-work of M. Molier who showed himself as always a horseman[4] full of elegance and knowledge.

A captivating resurrection of the forms of old-time[5] fencing was particularly interesting.

We had a festival with two sword-players of Louis XII in a bout with dag-

---

1. *tout-Paris*
2. *a fort goûté*
3. *la danse de l'aimé*
4. *écuyer*
5. Although the word used in the text is *ancienne*, it carries connotations of previous, no longer existing, and simply not current rather than necessarily of the remote past

ger and with cloak, the bout of Saint Georges with the Knight of Eon, executed with astonishing gusto by Mme M. Chevalier and M. Gueldry, and finally with a modern fencing lesson by Messrs Corthey and Vavasseur.

The various elements of these presentations, so well combined, charmed a first class public who did not stop applauding with enthusiasm the artists and their director to whom one owes such attractive evenings.

The sword: The Mignons: dagger and sword (1606) | Swiss and Scots of the Guard of Louis XII: two-handed sword | Jarnac and Châteignerie (under Henry II): sword and buckler | Saint George and the Knight of Eon (1787): the French school | Modern fencing

1. Giralda, horse jumper | 2. Clowns | 3. Feathered equestrian entertainment | 4. The African dance, Mlle Rivolta | 5. The Sword | 6. Buffalo and Ostrich, a fantasy | 7. Dressage (M. Adrien Marie)
*The evening of 11 June at the Circus Molier | Fencing in Different Periods | Exercises | (Drawings by M. Adrien Marie)*

# A Clown's Report from the Circus Molier

*Revue Illustrée*, June 1887, pp.32-3

From 8 o'clock, the area around the stage and all the boxes were occupied, conquered by shining society; not a single corner empty. Here and there, in the picturesque decor of a plaza in Murcie,[1] gentlemen in black attire, clinging to the wall, seated uncertainly on architectural projections, in the most amusing postures seeking, for better or worse, to maintain their balance. Others were perched on ladders, leaned on windows where, in the grace of their beauty and the glory of appearance, smiled friendly ladies.

Some intimates, mixing with the artists in costume, installed themselves in the patron's box which overlooks the stables. There, there was among others, M. De La Rochefoucault, in a grey harlequin suit.[2] He will have his sensational number — a new work of aerial acrobatics — which ends the third part. Waiting, from there, he regards the spectacle, the spectacle on the stage, where two swordsmen[3] under Louis XII, Messrs Boudius et Jeannency, one dressed as a Swiss and the other as a Scot of the king's guard, give with the two-handed sword a lesson and a bout; — the spectacle in the box where, arriving in the aisles of the circus, a troop of pretty women are obliged to climb the ladder and pass through a trapdoor[4] in order to mount to the upper boxes. There is, along the rafters in a rustle of precious fabrics, lace, cambric, the passage of tiny feet shod in ravishing slippers of silk, of legs which raise the lowly to joy — pardon, of silk[5] — semi-transparent. As the clown who awaits his number, I have in my eye all these pretty feet; and the calves which ascend lose themselves — interruptions of lines harmonious minxes — in the crowd of skirts.

However, the two brothers, Messrs Breittmayer, continue in scholarly and easy silhouettes the reconstruction of the history of fencing. In Jarnac and Châtaignerie, using sword and buckler according to the Italian school, they portray a bout under Henry II. Next, the baron Rivet and the count of Vissocq, as Les Mignons, still according to the Italian style, battle with infinite gusto and skill with dagger and cloak.

It is the turn of the French school, so correct, so fine. Just a century apart,

1. A tourist town on the Mediterranean coast of Spain
2. *en complete gris de carreaux*
3. *joueurs d'épée*
4. *une trappe de pigeonnier*
5. A play on words between the rhymes *joie* (joy) and *soie* (silk); the joke doesn't survive translation

Mme Mathilde Chevalier and M. Victor Gueldry give us the illusion of the bout which took place 8 April 1787, between Saint-Georges and the Knight of Eon. It is perfect, impeccable. The salute, very pleasant to see with sword and tricorne, is executed marvelously. The Knight of Eon, superb of form in black shirt, skirt tucked in on the side, forces applause in a succession of beautiful armed stances. Finally, Messrs Corthey and Vavasseur, who present modern fencing, cross foils; and soon the bravos bring down the circus, while in the patron's box, on the ladder which leads to the loft from where they could see through a crack, climb again the two "actresses" that we had forgotten were there,[6] four tiny feet, four agile calves which, on stage, with clicks of steel — the contrary[7] song, dapper and wild, of the sword — accompany the triumph.

Mlle d'Yvrès shows Giralda, a jumping mare, after which, there is an entry of clowns by Mlles Briege and Menty. The effects of the shirts, the two clownesses, make tremble with desire and raise the temperature of the hands of the spectators, who all wield opera glasses at Menty above all, the blonde with her body thin but so Parisian. Molier is admired by all the connoisseurs in the equestrian refrain, secular and non obligatory.[8] Mlle Walberg presents with success Sabatka, a horse of the high school, and Yvanoff, the jumper. M. Van Huysen juggles with weights of 50 kilos. M. Adrien Marie, disguised on Cabrion who carries in a crouch Mme Pipelet,[9] makes, on a horse at the gallop, the portraits of the prettiest women in society; all are recognised.

And strange musicians, black as ebony, enter in procession onto the stage, dressed picturesquely. They crouch on the oriental carpets and whisper chants, pinching the strings of their banjos, hitting the donkey skins, breathing on bamboo flutes. Descending from the camel which brought her, Mlle Rivolta, former dancer with the Eden-Theatre, delicate under her gauze veil, begins a belly dance,[10] a dance of the belly in lascivious attitudes, with eyes lost and blank. It has had much success, the "Little Louis", as we called Mlle Rivolta at 16 years old. The tribe of Beny-ben-Ouville[11] made its deafeningly savage cry, rhythmic and continuous, and, ears strained, muzzle in the air, the camel nodded.

After the remarkable gymnastics of Messrs Rivet and Vavasseur, two comic attempts on the stage and a moving athletic battle, here an intermission by Mlle

---

6. *on ne savait plus où fourrer* - we no longer knew where to hide
7. *antithétique*
8. *la equestre scie, laïque et non obligatoire*
9. Characters from the famous and popular novel, <u>Les Mystères de Paris</u>
10. *une danse d'aimée* - specifically a dance imagined to be of ancient Egypt
11. The Circus Molier was located on the rue Benouville, Paris

Dezoder, from the Palais Royal and the illustrator Gerbault, who, the white-faced unhooker of the stars in his role of clown, showed a lively aesthetic originality.

The penultimate diversion, Plumeau, is an original operation directed by Molier. The horsemen, in a number with the inventor of their costumes, Adrien Marie, directed by the completely ravishing Miss Pâquerette, are extremely funny[12] and when they charge, the feathers[13] in front, terrible. Finally, M. Hubert de la Rochefoucauld, in a soft green shirt, goes from a first trapeze to a second, from one end of the circus to the other, making perilous leaps. But, with such skill, it is not astonishing that he always achieves his destination.

The diabolical hour, midnight. Battalions of trend-setters and high dandies[14] expand onto the stage. The legendary narrow stairs which lead to the boxes are worse than the corridor of the Opera under the clock on nights of the grand ball. Everywhere there are signals, teasing gallants, while numerous servants bring, even on the stage, prepared dinners on little tables. The champagne flows, laughter rings out like sparkling wine and the picture is unexpectedly petty. From here, from there, the worldly grooms, in white trousers and red vest, a fleet of blue ribbons on the left shoulder, a clown in red fur, a black clown, a white clown, a Pierette, the "ebony whistle" whom the powder greys a little, women in low-cut attire, that the swirling dances has, in the corners, dusted with powder. Molier who, with consummate skill has made his love of horses fashionable, goes from group to group. We acclaim, all together, the young director, who announces a surprise. "My children, as you have been so good, we will show you the magic lantern."

There is, the gas crowns are almost extinguished, a series of comic scenes of the Restoration and in time M. —— explains them with infinite humour. Next, there are portraits of artists, from the owner to the Duke of——, dressed, gardenia in his buttonhole, "armed from head to toe," said the manager, not without irony, "ready to leave for the battle of the flowers." The magic lantern ends, the dance takes up anew; the party is at its best, if not at its worst. And I think of the masterpiece a painter could make – a deep, a profound, an elegant Parisian artist, in love with his time – in doing it. But, this time, it would be of the truly superficial life, anxious and overexcited — the lone painting of couture: the Romans in decadence. People of the nobility, of fortune, of talent, girls, all are brought together here, merit, youth, beauty; and — Balzac, my old friend, you have made that masterpiece — it is the synthesis of Parisian comedy.

12. *infiniment drole*
13. *un plumeau* is a feather duster but I'm not entirely certain that is the meaning intended here
14. *de gimmeuses et de hauts gommeux*

*To copy, comply with: Félicien Champsaur*

# The Society for the Advancement of Fencing

*La Grande Dame*, 1894 (A2), pp.97-100

>  Do not draw me without reason,
>  Do not return me without honour.

The antique Castilian device, that which the knight of legend inscribed in gold letters on his loyal Toledo blade, serves today as the emblem of the Society for the Advancement of Fencing, for this Society whose noble efforts have revived the cult of the sword and have put again in great honour this weapon with such a beautiful French tradition.[1]

Presided over by M. H. de Villeneuve, the Society for the Advancement of Fencing is one of the more ancient among societies of this type : the fencing hall,[2] where have begun and where have trained the best fencers of this time, uniting not only the great professionals, the masters, that is to say the classics, whose training and skill are universal, but also the amateurs, the fans of the blade, the personalities in the view of the world of fencing, the celebrities[3] of the sword.

The legitimate affection enjoyed by the Society is acknowledged whenever in public ceremony, in official bouts, its members offer their solemn performance: the festival of the foil.

This year, the program offers a further attraction: the historical reconstruction, minutely documented, of the duel from the sixteenth century, the period in which fencing properly called begins (ruled by Henri II) until our days.

Five bouts, where the costumes, weapons, attitudes, the play — directed by M. Corthey with true wisdom[4] — achieved for the spectators the perfect illusion of bygone periods, of lost chivalry, of those heroic times where our imagination sees again the stories of adventure, the reknowned follies, the fights and epic struggles : Alexandre Dumas, le Pré-aux-Clercs, the Mignons, the musketeers, the captains of the long rapier and moustache in the wind,[5] the bully lying in wait in dark alleys for the late-coming bourgeois, Saltabadil, Don César,

---

1. *d'une si belle tradition française*
2. *salle d'armes*
3. *le Tout-Paris*
4. *avec une veritable science*
5. *à moustache au vent*

58  Fencing through the Ages

Cyrano, Bussy, Saint-Georges, all these charming heroes of dreams and history, all these exquisite figures lost in the greyness of the centuries.

With Messrs Bottet and Joseph Renaud, there is the two-handed sword against the sword and buckler; there is Jarnac and Chataigneraie; there is the formidable weapon handled by the Swiss with muscles of steel and with which the subtle Italians make a learned and treacherous fencing.

Messrs G. Andrieu and Weber-Halouin revived the reign of Henri III, the Mignons : Quelus, Schomberg, Maugiron, refined of honour, made-up, perfumed with amber, pretty and preened; the fight with hands armed:

> With sword and dagger, in worthy gentlemen
> As befits when one is from the house which we are from.

Modern boxing – with, in place of the vulgar punch, the iron of the dagger and sword – gives just enough idea of this fencing where the passes, voltes, leaps, the solidity and agility of the legs hold the premier place.

We are under Louis XIII with Messrs De Laborie and Saint-Chéron. They simulate the meeting of a musketeer of His Eminence with a scout,[6] one of the cutthroats like one sees surge, between the dog and the wolf, around the Louvre and the Pont-Nuef. The fencing in this period became wise and disengaged tangibly from the Italian tradition. One employs frequently the cape, the dagger, but these are no longer but the vestiges of an art which begins to have its principles and classic strikes. This minute and difficult reconstruction, due to the research which certainly had been laborious, give the greatest honour to M. Corthey.

Finally, the hook of the evening was the bout of the Knight of Eon, the famous Knight of Eon, depicted by Mme. Gabriel, with a teacher (the Knight of Saint-Georges) depicted by M. Gabriel. M. Gabriel is the former master of arms of Saint-Cyr; Mme. Gabriel is the instructor of the Women's Fencing Circle,[7] newly founded. In those two, they have created for themselves a Parisian notoriety and the fencing world has legitimately assigned them the place which they deserve in the hierarchy of professional fencers.

With Saint-Georges, French fencing arrives at its complete development and in the nineteenth century, with La Boëssière junior, it attained the proportions of an exact science. The use of the square blade and of the foil becomes

---

6. *un batteur d'estrade* - a beater of the way
7. *Cercle d'escrime des dames*

general. It is the classic period : swordplay[8] becomes an art with absolute rules, laws, glorious traditions, masters, instructors, academies.

The duel is no longer an adventurous meeting in some isolated corner without witnesses, without regular assistance to catch the treacherous, the assassin, the criminal. The duel has its code and despite its detractors, its enemies, despite the philosophers in tirades and in glasses,[9] it has implanted itself officially in custom. It becomes, in delicate or serious circumstances of life, the unique means of reparation or vengeance imposed on people of honour.

Yet the sword is a symbol, a symbol of right, of bravery, of serene loyalty. To carry the sword under the Ancien Regime was sign of nobility. In the Crusades, the handle of the sword was depicted as a cross. It touched of the lips of the dying knight.[10] Against the formidable squares of Spanish infantry, the King's Bodyguard,[11] throwing down the pistols drew the sword[12] and advance in avalanche on the plains of Fontenoy: "Secure your hats, masters," said the field marshall. "We will have the honour of charging." And on each page of the history of France, almost on each line, it is the sword, it is the fine blade of steel, it is the flexible stem of iron which recounts the conquests, the chivalric epics, the loyal and marvelous combat. The celebration of the sword is a French celebration and one should warmly congratulate M. de Villeneuve and his friends for having so well and beautifully given us this event.

The performance was finished by a modern bout between Messrs Cloudier and Doumic, of relatively little interest, and a concert where several artists of the Opera and the Théâtre-Francais were heard.

*Jean de Mitty*

---

8. *le jeu de l'épée*
9. *à tirades et à lunettes* – the meaning is unclear
10. *chevalier agonisant*
11. *la maison du roi*
12. *mettait l'épée au clair*

# Letter from Belgium

*Le Figaro*, 16 May 1894, p.3

*[Unrelated topical news from Belgium removed]*

Next Monday,[1] another fete of active interest – but we won't go to it – given in Brussels at the *Scène de la Monnaie*: "Fencing Through the Ages", drawn in characteristic scenes composed for the event with dialogued episodes.

This event[2] is organised by the Press Committee. The idea was suggested to the president of the Committee, our brother M. Gustave Lemaire, by a session of old-time fencing given about three months ago at the Grand Hotel of Paris and earlier in *Le Figaro*. M. Georges Eekhoud was responsible for composing this scenario here:

1st – The Judgement of God in the Middle Ages – a city in the time of King Childebert;

2nd – Sir Jacques Lalaing – single combat in the marketplace of Bruges under Philippe-le-Bon;

3rd – Venetian Fantasy – Venice in the 15th century; the Plaza San-Marco and the Lido;

4th – An adventure of Alexandre Farnese – an attack of cutthroats[3] at a crossroads at Plaisance;

5th – Under Henry III – a meeting in a court of the Louvre between the people of the King and those of the Guises;

6th – Flesh for Crows – an altercation between musketeers in a street in Compeigne under Louis XIII;

7th – Supper at Carmargo's Place – a duel under Louis XV;

1. Refers to 21 May 1894
2. *cérémonie*
3. *coupe-jarrets*

8th – A bout between the Knight of Eon and Angelo.

Figuring in this series of historical bouts: M. et Mme Gabriel of Paris and several English fencers, the best blades of the United Kingdom belonging to the London Rifle Brigade, among others Captain Alfred Hutton, a scholar as well as a practitioner, who has made a speciality of historical fencing.

The music of the spectacle has been composed by Messrs de Greef, Gilson, Leon Dubois and Soubre, who have interleaved ancient melodies in their compositions. Various artists of our theatres and students of the Conservatory are responsible for the dialogue part under the intelligent direction of M. Candeilh, former director of the Parc Theatre.

Thus, certainly, an original event and [one] which will have as much success as the famous tournament given at the Hotel-de-Ville. We add that it has been organised with a charitable aim whose nature will further enhance its merit.[4]

*[Unrelated topical news from Belgium removed]*

---

4. *ce qui est de nature à en rehausser encore le mérite*

# On the Subject of the Transformation of the Combat Sword

Adolphe Corthey
2nd edition
Paris
Printed: G. Camproger,
52 rue de Provence
1895

---

**From the same author**

| | |
|---|---:|
| Foil and épée, a study | 1 fr |
| French and Prussians: Sidearms and Firearms 2nd edition | 1 fr |
| A small treatise on fencing with the bayonet, 2nd edition | 1 fr |

**To appear shortly**

Fencing through the Ages, 1 volume

---

*Minutes of the meeting of the Committee of 12 January 1894 at which this report was read and approved.*

For a certain number of years, the manner of fighting in the field, the play of the duel, has preoccupied a great number of fencers and captivated the fencing halls.

Strangely enough, all concern themselves greatly with the manner of fighting. We have not seen them concern themselves with the weapon of combat.

Nonetheless, it is always this latter which made the former.

And if logic says it to us, the facts prove it to us.

Passing beyond Marozzo and the other Italian authors who parried with the buckler then with the sword and the left hand or the dagger, beyond still Saint-Didier who only employed the left hand unarmed and Thibault who uses the great quillions of the Spanish sword, we arrive at Besnard, Liancourt and the other masters of the period of Louis XIV who parried with the sword blade. We see that in the strikes as in the parries their play is constrained by the form of this blade which is flat, with or without stops, with or without fullers.

For example: they knew perfectly the *contres* but they did not employ them in the bout. They only used them as a lesson to exercise the hand.

The same constrained play, with only some variation, continues during the 18th century with Danet, Angelo, etc, and it is only in the 19th century, after the invention of the square bladed foil, that La Boëssière created modern fencing, this almost mathematical science with its powerful parries without effort, varied in all lines, passing from simple parries to *contres*, from the *tac à l'enveloppement*, from the envelopment to the *opposition*; this refined art with its attack strikes of nearly absolute safety and its feints of incomparable subtlety.

We are justified therefore to say that it is much less fencing which made the weapon than the weapon which made fencing.

And we could add that the history of fencing is but the history of the sword.

Today, after so much perfection and progress, we still use two weapons (we do not speak, it goes without saying, of those which are used in war), the one, the late comer, which is the creation of the 19th century, we preserve for the salle, for entertainment, for the art; this is the square foil. The other, more ancient and which is a legacy of the 18th century, we use for the duel; this is the triangular épée.

For people outside of fencing, this matters little.

A foil, an épée, a square blade, a triangular blade, it is still a weapon which stabs, is it not? While we can make a [blade edge of] greater or lesser angle, to what end is all this geometry![1]

For you, sirs, experienced practitioners, you have so well understood that this question, frivolous in appearance, was of capital importance to the fencing point of view that, at once, you appointed some among you to examine the modifications to bring to the weapon currently in use in the field.

These modifications seem to us in reality simple enough, since they would limit themselves to bringing back, as much as possible, to the form of the weapon of the duel, the weapon of the salle, the épée from the foil.

Currently, the one is very different to the other: the blade of the first is triangular, that of the second is square; the latter is fullered, the former is filled.

The strike of the épée blade presents, in effect, a triangle of which the base is discernibly larger than the two other sides.

It has therefore a deformed aspect, since, in reality, it would be flat, if it was not adorned with a type of protuberance.

Because of the manner in which it is mounted in the guard position, the base of the triangle is found therefore turned upwards, the shallowest angle downwards.

From this form and from this disposition arise some very serious consequences for the parry, the riposte and the attack.

Concerning the parry, first the circular movements, and by consequence the counters, are difficult, nearly as difficult as if the blade was completely flat, since it has in any case much more width than thickness. It follows, even the simple *tac* or opposition lacks safety, authority and power, since in *sixte* it is the base of the triangle, that is to say the flat surface, which meets the opposing weapon and that in *tierce* and in *quarte* it is the least prominent angle.

It is for the same reason that the envelopments are nearly impossible with the current épée.

Regarding the ripostes and attacks, they equally lack safety, always for the same cause.

Thus, the weapon which we use in the duel is not worth even the flat sword with one or two edges, the third angle of the blade serving absolutely only to prevent it cutting. We can even add that a simple rifle ramrod would be superior since this latter would present if not a larger authority of opposition at least greater ease in circular movements.

From this collection of faults in the weapon, a limited and incomplete art results which lacks not only elegance but, more seriously, safety.

We wanted to make a new invention under the name *field play*. We ultimately found only a primitive play.

---

1. *Alors que peut nous faire un angle de plus ou de moins et à quoi bon toute cette géométrie!*

The so-called inventors, not able to do with their antiquated instrument that which we can do in the salle with the modern foil, present themselves as fencing reformers, that is to say, they acted as armourers who insert a beautiful and strong sword in a small scabbard, for preserving this scabbard grinds the sword.

They said, modify the art. We say, modify the weapon.

Taking the foil as the starting point, we will choose a square and very strong blade, close to the thickness of that of the épée. If we fuller the four faces, the weapon that we obtain will be rigid like the épée and handy like the foil, since as in the latter, the thickness will be equal to the width.

As in the latter equally, the edges,[2] placed at equal distance, will permit nothing to change in the attacks and in the parries.

We think, in effect, that it is the disposition of the edges which gives the opposition its safety, power, lightness and bite at once.

We can however take account of the way in which the parry is formed in examining one of these foils which has been in the hands of a teacher for a long time. The part of the blade which constitutes the forte has become completely rounded and resembles the shaft of a feather.

This indicates that, in the rotation of the wrist to parry, this pivot is always made on two edges, be they in *quarte*, in *tierce* or in *sixte*.

We see therefore if the consequences of the proposed transformation could be considered from the point of view of the play, the transformation itself, from the point of view of the form of the blade, is reduced to little since we have already the Lebel bayonet[3] which is a quadrangular weapon with four fullers.

The only difference that it would present with the new épée (the width put aside, of course) consists in the disposition of the edges. That, moreover, is only a matter of mounting the blade on the handle.

We do not want to conclude without dealing with[4] an objection which has been presented against the use of the foil in the field (the only, moreover) and that we would renew perhaps in this regard with the proposed weapon.

Strangely enough, this objection, formulated as a question of fencing, is drawn from the medical arena.

One claims that the foil injury was more dangerous than that of the épée; the blood in one case being re-absorbed more easily inside the body than in the other by the fact of the small dimension of the opening.

---

2. lit: the angles, used in this manner several times below
3. Refers to the Fusil Modèle 1886 M93 called the "Fusil Lebel"
4. *sans aller devant*

Some surgeons of high rank have affirmed to us the opposite and we know of numerous examples including a very recent one in favour of their opinion.

But we will not enter into this medical controversy which is not our responsibility and whose possible consequences would be to demonstrate that the smaller the wound, the greater the danger.

We will confine ourselves to note first that one goes not on the field with the aim of frolicking and, if the causes of the duel must always be serious, we do not concern ourselves if the injuries which follow are more or less light.

Finally, that the dimensions if not the form of the new épée, should not be significantly different to those of the previous, the medical discussion remains as is and that, by consequence, we do not have to worry about it.

Considering therefore the current play, called in the field, is notably different to that which one does in the salle and which constitutes modern fencing, that this restrained play, is largely due to the use of an outdated and obviously defective weapon; that the use of a new weapon, more in harmony with the progress of fencing, would cause to disappear in part the very damaging antagonism which exists between the two plays; considering finally that a sword with a square blade and four fullers appears to attain this goal.

We have the honour to propose to the Committee to issue the desire that in all meetings the weapon currently in use be replaced by the sword indicated above.

---

*The wish of the Committee is in part realised. The sword which, at the moment of its vote, existed only in a theoretical state is now fabricated and is found on the market.*

*The new square blade and with four fullers has the width of the previous. Its maximum thickness at the heel is nine and a half millimetres. It weighs approximately 490 grams.*

www.ingramcontent.com/pod-product-compliance
Lightning Source LLC
Chambersburg PA
CBHW032050090426
42744CB00004B/156